≪ Seven Times Down ≫

Poems & Prose
by
Wilfred Hildonen

Seven Times Down
by Wilfred Hildonen
First Edition Paperback
Printed in the U.S.A.

ISBN: 979-8-88526-256-9

Published by **Cajun Mutt Press**

Introduction

Please allow me to introduce myself. I'm a nobody from no place special. I was born on the edge of the inhabitable world, up in the Arctic part of Norway, up where the three tribes meet, as they say. The name of the river rolling by my birthplace says it all. It's Tana and it's Deatnu and it's Teno. It depends on who you ask; Norwegian, Sámi or Finn. I am two out of the three, because I am only Norwegian by birthplace and maybe not even that, because the land didn't belong to them, but to the Sámi and a Finnish tribe called the Kveni. Well, not even to them, because the idea that a piece of land belongs to somebody is a peculiar one, if you think about it. I guess it has to do with what Cain did to Abel.

Speaking of which, I'm also a religious atheist and a non-conformist traditionalist. I work as a professional court jester, only the court belongs to the common man and woman today, not the King. In other words, I'm a political cartoonist. And an artist. A writer and a poet. I'm an autodidact when it comes to everything and I don't belong to any group, simply because I don't fit in any.

I don't care too much about art or poetry or literature as a consumer. Oh, I consume it when I encounter it, but mostly if I visit a gallery, I leave disappointed. When I read a book, I often begin writing one in my head, but if I try to get it published, I'm being rejected, refused entry into Parnassus. Through this, I knock at its gates again.

I create what I do because I need to do it. Something in me wants to get out and it doesn't care in what form or fashion. Louis Armstrong once said that there are only two kinds of music - good and bad. That goes for all kinds of art, only I have begun to think it's actually splitting it up too much. There is only one kind of art.

Art.

What's important is not the form, but that which tries to express itself through the artist and the artist is a slave to that and only that and is therefore obliged to obey. There are no other rules.

These texts are in two languages, some of them, English and Norwegian. Some of them are written in English from the start, and some in Norwegian. English has been my second soul, since I learnt it at the age of eleven. I got Norwegian through my father and my mother, whose first language was Finnish, though, while my paternal grandparents spoke Sámi between themselves. Neither of my parents bothered to bring those two languages down to me, alas, because it was believed back then that it would be to my disadvantage.

I'm no longer a Norwegian citizen. Instead I carry a Finnish passport, although inside of me, in my heart, I am at least half Portuguese after more than a dozen years in Portugal, although my Brazilian wife protests and wants me to be her Viking, although I am no such thing. But

have you heard the one
about when a poet and a painter
a juggler a jester and a clown
went into a bar
together with a commoner
a prince a frog and a toad
a wizard and a demon
a saint and a devil
god himself and his mother
and a tramp and a stranger
a layabout and an idler
a blacksmith and a thief
a hustler and a beggar
an innocent and a sinner
a braggart and a drinker
a doer and a thinker
and how they all came out
as one
Man?

Table of Contents

Table of Contents

Seven Times Down

Poems & Prose
by
Wilfred Hildonen

I am

i am the one who believes in dreams
and who climbs to the top of the mountain
and who listens to the ocean
looking for eternity
in a grain of sand

and when i have reached the top of the mountain
i am the one who longs for the water of the ocean

Jeg er

jeg er den som tror på drømmer
og som klatrer opp på alle fjell
jeg er den som lytter til havets sang
og som søker etter evighet
i et korn av sand

jeg er den som oppe på fjellet
lengter etter havets salte vann

The holy grail

you seek the holy grail
and thought it would be a walk in the park
you're looking for light
and shun the dark
but tell me how
you will make it through the night
you believe in peace
and will never touch the sword
but how will you survive the fight
you want to save your soul
and leave body and matter behind
since the solution lies within
which sounds very fine
but I cannot see
how it sets us free
you want to be pure
and talk about love
but it doesn't involve
any other
and can you tell
how you will carry your soul
around
without the chalice
that your body is?

Den hellige gral

du søker den hellige gral
og trodde det var som en tur i parken
du leter etter lys
og unngår mørket
men fortell meg hvordan
du vil klare deg gjennom natta
du tror på fred
og vil aldri røre sverdet
men hvordan vil du overleve kampen
du vil frelse din sjel
og la kropp og materie ligge
fordi løsningen finnes i vårt indre
og det høres veldig bra ut
men jeg kan ikke se
hvordan det vil gjøre oss frie
du vil være ren
og snakker om kjærlighet
som ikke involverer noen andre
så kan du fortelle meg
hvordan vil du bære din sjel
uten den kalken
som ditt legeme er?

Seven Times Down

life goes up and life goes down
then it turns all around
and it will let you down
make you feel like a clown
you go seven times down
but you get eight times up

i sit and stare at the leaden sky
yesterday i felt eight miles high
i was so happy i sure could fly
but it was all a bloody lie
it's been said over and over again
what goes up must come down
and the higher you fly
the harder you hit the ground
it's a natural law
that makes life go round and round
and when you're on top
the next thing you know
you're crawling on the ground
crying like a goddamn' fool
life goes up and life goes down
and then it turns all around
and you go seven times down
but you get eight times up
you go seven times down
but you come eight times up
seven times down
but eight times up!

I do not belong

I do not belong. I have never belonged
I am a stranger here

I do not belong to any confined place, surrounded by walls and borders
I do not possess anything
I have borrowed the objects surrounding me
I do not belong to any religious belief
I do not belong to any ideology
I do not belong to any genre
I am not faithful
I do not swear allegiance to no one
no state
no person.
I do not accept any borders
I do not accept any limitations
I do not obey orders
I do not belong to anyone and no one belongs to me
I do not belong to my mother nor my father, not to my sisters nor my brothers
Not to my children nor their mothers.
They do not belong to me
I am not faithful. I will never be

Places have marked me
People have marked me
Cultures have marked me
Nature has marked me
I have been shaped by all of this, but I do not belong to any of it
I do not belong to my past and my future do not belong to me
My time is borrowed from eternity

I do belong
I belong to the first warm wind in spring
I belong to the billowing sea
I belong to fat flies crawling on a table in the heat of the sun
I belong to the ants, awakening after a long, cold winter
I belong to the horizon

It all belongs to me and I give it away for free
I belong to the world
I belong to the Universe from whence I came and
to which I shall return.
I am on the move
When time comes I shall move on
I do not run away
for I carry my burden with me
It belongs to me
and I belong to it

I am a wanderer
a nomad
and a tramp
I am the loose end
to you rigor
I am

Yin Yang

Soft arc red lips
Searching warm scent of skin
Gentle circle encompassing soft arc
Tearful smile hidden in golden hair
Skin hissing against skin
Hard muscles against tense muscles
Vibrating in sharp Zs
Tender fingers gently glide across long arcs
Of electrically charged Zs
Meandering upwards
Upwards
into the darkness above
The young handsome boy
Climbs up the spiral
While the old fakir
Conjures up lonely trills
The boy disappears into the dark
The audience let out a breathless gasp
The sound of hard blows and hoarse cries from above
Blood rains down on playing fair children's hair
Up from the ground comes the young and pretty boy
Climbing up a golden helix
Of electrically charged Zs
Disappearing into the darkness above
The audience laughs out of relief
Which soon is transformed into screams of horror
And hysterical crying
When blood rains down again
Over fair children's hair
Reports of a war arrive
And people cry
The war turns into peace
And people laugh
Weeping clowns dance in the circus ring
Throwing up clouds of dust
In the sharp spotlight

The audience laugh relieved
And clap hands in excitement
With tears in their eyes
While children cry and shout:
They don't have clothes on!
The audience smile indulgently
While the emperor weeps
And the slaves laugh
The young poet looks across the sea
While the surf rolls unseen towards his eyes
The dense fog thunders silently on the horizon
Revealing a rolling moon
For eyes which didn't see
Refugees on display marching slowly
Across flickering blue TV-screens
To the sound of silver spoons
Clinking against delicate china
And the conversation flows
above crumbs of cake

The imploring eyes of a dog
Create melancholic amusement

Yin Yang

rød munns myke buer
søker huds varme duft
myke sirkler omslutter myke buer
og gyldent hår gjemmer tårer i et smil
mens hud hvisler mot hud
harde muskler mot spente muskler
sitrer med skarpe z'er
og ømme fingre løper følsomt over lange buer
med elektrisk ladete z'er
som slynger seg oppover
oppover
mot mørket ovenfor
den unge vakre gutten
klatrer opp langs spiralen
mens den gamle fakiren
tryller fram ensomme triller
før gutten forsvinner i mørket
og publikum gisper åndeløst
før lyden av harde slag og hese skrik høres ovenfra
og blodet regner over lekende barns lyse hår
men opp fra bakken kommer den unge vakre gutten
klatrende oppover en gylden spiral
av elektrisk ladete z'er
og forsvinner i mørket der oppe
mens publikum ler en befriende latter
som snart går over i skrekkslagne skrik
og hysterisk gråt
når blodet regner igjen
over lekende barns lyse hår
meldinger om en krig kommer
og folket gråter
krigen går over i fred
og folket ler
klovnene danser gråtende rundt i manesjen
og hvirvler opp skyer av støv
i det skarpe rampelyset

menneskene ler overgivent
og klapper begeistret i hendene
med tårefylte øyne
mens barn gråter og roper
de har jo ikke klær!
tilskuerne ler overbærende
mens keiseren gråter
og trellene ler
den unge poeten ser utover havet
mens bølgene ruller usette mot øynene hans
den tette tåken tordner lydløst i horisonten
og avslører en rullende måne
for øyne som ikke så noenting
flyktningparader ruller langsomt over
blå TV-skjermer
til akkompagnement av sølvskjeer
mot flortynt porselen
og konversasjonen løper
lett og lekende over kakesmuler
mens hundens saktmodige øyne
skaper en vemodig glede

A poem for a doomsday

Don't lose faith
You who carry a heavy load
Don't lose your mind
When you'll be whirled around
When the night becomes dark and deep
And all hope will be whisked away
Don't lose faith
Although the Earth will shake
And mountains will tremble
Dark clouds will rise
Tempest will rage
Thunder will crash
And lightning will flash
All false hopes
Will be put to shame
Don't be afraid
When the horizon fades
Don't lose faith
Through the darkest of nights
When life withers away
In an endless drought

Soon the sky will be rent asunder
With a thundering crash
And the light will burn
Through every ceiling
The rain will flood
And all will come to be
And he who was last
Will be the first
And your thirst
Shall be quenched

Dommedagsdikt

mist ikke motet
dere som bærer tungt
tap ikke hodet
når dere hvirvles rundt
når natten blir dyp og mørk
og alt håp blåser bort
så mist ikke motet
selv om jorden ryster og fjellene skjelver
og skybankene tårner seg opp

stormen vil rase
og torden vil rulle
lynene vil flamme
og alle falske håp
vil bli gjort til skamme

men bli ikke redde
når horisonten viskes ut
mist ikke motet
i det tette mørket
mist ikke motet
selv om livet visner
i en endeløs tørke

snart vil himmelen revne
med tordnende brak
og lyset vil brenne
gjennom stengende tak
regnet vil flomme
og slukke din sviende tørst
alt vil komme
og den som var sist
skal være først

Wet dream

A slowly growing swell
Carries me along a golden beach
The water is azure
Yellow butterflies dancing on the breeze
And Aphrodite raises up from the waves
With white stripes of foam
Running down her body golden brown
A flurry of hot emotions
Cascading through my newborn throat

Every tone and every song
Streaming through me
Drive me towards her golden body
And the sea currents carry her shell
Across the cyan-coloured deep

Våt drøm

Langsomt rullende dønninger
bærer meg av gårde langs gyldne strender
havet er asurblått
og gule sommerfugler leker i den høye luften
afrodite stiger opp av havet
mens hvite strimer av skum
renner nedover den nakne, gyllenbrune kroppen
mens en kaskade av hete følelser
strømmer gjennom min nyfødte strupe

hver tone og hver sang
som er til
strømmer gjennom meg
og driver meg mot afrodites varme kropp
og havstrømmene fører skjellet hennes
av gårde
over blågrønne dybder

White sand in blue darkness

White sand shines in blue darkness
Footprints cast dark shadows
Disappearing in the distance
Statues made of cold grey steel
Have their backs turned
Towards a lonely wanderer in the night
And skulking in the grey haze
A figure comes closer
Vague like eternity itself

Hvit sand i blått mørke

hvit sand lyser i blått mørke
fotspor kaster mørke skygger
forsvinner i det fjerne
statuer av iskaldt grått stål
står med ryggen vendt
mot en ensom vandrer i natten
og smygende i den grå disen
kommer en skikkelse
uklar som evigheten selv

Wildflowers

If your days are so dark
And your nights so cold
If you feel battered, defeated and old
Why keep rambling on?
Why not leave the stage
call it a day and go away?

My reason to go on
is that wildflowers return
And as long as wildflowers return
there's magic abound
As long as wildflowers return
Come rain come flood
When wildflowers return
we survive the spill of blood.

My only reason to go on is this
that wildflowers return.
Days may be dark and nights may be cold
I have gambled and I lost in the game of love
I have no faith in the powers that be
not here below nor in heavens above
But as long as wild flowers do return
there is my reason to go on.
As long as wildflowers return
Nothing left to explain
As long as wildflowers return
like those which withered and died
As long as wildflowers return
dressed in beauty
with a scent of future
and hope beyond reason
I will ramble on for yet another season.
As long as wildflowers return
I need no more and crave no less
that wildflowers return.

Ville blomster

hvis dagene dine er så mørke
og natta di er så svart
og hvis du føler deg rundjult
nedslått og trøtt
hvorfor holder du stadig på?
hvorfor ikke forlate scenen
og si at nok er nok
og bare gå din vei?

men den eneste grunnen
jeg har å stå på
er den at ville blomster vender tilbake
som om det var magi med i spillet

så lenge ville blomster kommer tilbake
så må det regne og må det storme
i førti dager til ende
for så lenge ville blomster kommer igjen
vil vi overleve blodet som spilles
så lenge ville blomster kommer tilbake
holder vi ut

dagene er mørke og nettene kalde
og jeg satset alt jeg hadde
og tapte det alt sammen
i det store kjærlighetsspillet
og jeg tror ikke på høyere makter
hverken her nede eller høyt der oppe
men så lenge ville blomster kommer tilbake
så er det grunn nok for meg til å stå på
så lenge ville blomster kommer igjen

Atrocities in darkness

Things occur in darkness
Brains violate their thoughts
Iron-shod heels trample on transparent souls
The breaking wheel awaits the innocents
who walk on the path of peace
Thoughts which do not conform
Are being whipped and chained
Hands doing what they were meant for
Are lowered into molten lead
Trains pass through the night
Filled with prisoners in chains
Found guilty of looking for love
And dreaming of opportunity
All and everyone are thrown
Down into the grey maelstrom
Of conformity
And the door to the mystery room
Is locked and lovers are exiled
forced to live on cold and lonely plains
Covered with ice

Things occur in darkness
And a volcano of hate grows underground
An avenger is coming tonight
Blood is boiling
And there is a fire that burns
Through the clouds in the sky

Down on the beach
A child is lost

Ting som skjer i mørket

ting skjer i mørket
hjerner voldtar sine egne tanker
jernhæler tramper på transparente sjeler
steile og hjul venter de naive som vandrer på fredsveien
tanker som ikke har den rette formen
blir pisket og lagt i lenker
og hender som gjør hva de ble skapt for
blir senket ned i smeltet bly
det går fangetransporter om natta
fulle med folk som våget å søke
etter mangfold og kjærlighet
alt og alle kastes ned
i en grå og jevn malstrøm
og alle er nektet adgang
til mysterierommet
og de elskende blir forvist
til ensomme vidder dekket av is
ting skjer i mørket
og en vulkan av hat
vokser under bakken
og i natt er en hevner på vei
blodet koker
og himmelens skyer
bærer på en glødende ild
nede ved stranden
har et barn gått seg vill

All the roads which lead to roam

walking through the nightshade
walking through the moonscape
lights in the sky wink off and on
people gazing with unseen starlight in their eyes
drowsily wondering why

walking through purple haze
walking at the dark side of the moon
falling through empty space
listen to the howling of the wolves
gathering at the gates of dawn

behold the abundance of the world
behold the rich beauty of running blood
uncover your ears
turn to the screams rising from scorched soil
await the rise of the threatening flood

there's a shadow hidden in the secret of our dreams
invisible fingers reaching for the soft of our throats
footprints left by someone unknown
disappearing towards the horizon
laughter seeping through the cracks in the walls

when the sky trembles
don't look back
don't look around
when clouds depart
keep on walking
eyes to the ground
when lightning strikes
don't look back
don't look around

and all those roads which lead to roam
won't help you to find your way back home

By the Whipping Post

She knew he was up to no good as soon as she saw him approaching her. She had never seen him before and he was young and rather handsome, she thought, but she noticed that soft look he had in his eyes, just like they were covered by a humid film. Repulsive, she found it, obnoxious even.

He came right up to her and held out his hands and there it was! The thing. Pulsating and almost shapeless. It was covered all over by bright red and wet blood which kept dripping from his hands and down to the ground.

- I have come to give you my heart, he said in a soft and melodic voice.

- No! She reeled back in disgust, holding up her hands in front of her like she wanted to protect herself from an assault.

- Take that bloody thing away from me! she screamed, her voice almost failing her.

- I don't want anything of it! You hear me!

- B-but.... The young boy stuttered and looked at her with eyes dark with pain now and the film was turning into something fluid. She shut her eyes.

- Guards! she screamed at the top of her lungs, turning away from him.

The guards came running, their iron-heeled boots drumming against the ground.

- Take him to the whipping post! she demanded, pointing towards him.

- And get rid of that - that thing!

She didn't even bother to watch them as they executed her orders. She knew they would do as the law commanded. He would receive a hundred lashes. She walked hurriedly away and locked herself inside her chambers.

Later that night, she could not get to sleep. She tossed herself back and forth and she felt a strange, indefinable pain located somewhere around her abdomen. His face appeared in front of her when she closed her eyes and tried to fall asleep. In the end she realised that she must do something about it. She had to set him free in order to be able to sleep. She got up and dressed herself hurriedly and went out into the dark night and marched briskly towards the whipping post.

When she reached it, she couldn't believe her eyes. There was no one there! She could see how the ropes were still tied around the post, but their ends were cut with some sharp instrument and hung loose. Someone had dared to come to his rescue! She was almost stunned by the mere thought of it. Who could have been so brave?

She turned her back to the whipping post, knowing that she would not be able to sleep, furious inside because of it, but the fury was mixed with a feeling of sadness, like she had lost something near and dear. She frowned and clenched her fists and bit her lip until a drop of blood appeared. Just a tiny, single drop of blood.

A sunny song

Life is a heavy weight to carry around
So we need a sunny song
To help us getting along
How I wish I had a sunny song
to give to you to sing
About roses and kisses and
A love which never misses
and is always right
About flowers and a summertime's night
When fireflies are hissing
And nothing is missing
And all the bottles are full
And life is exciting and far from dull
A sunny song when life is good
And people are kind and mean well
I wish I had such a sunny song
To give to you to sing, but...
Oh well…

En solskinnslåt

Livet er tungt å bære rundt
så vi behøver en solskinnslåt
for å orke med alt
å, som jeg ønsker jeg hadde en solskinnslåt
som dere kunne synge til
om roser og kyss og klem
om en kjærlighet der jenta får sin gutt
om blomster og en midtsommerkveld
når ildfluer hvisler
og ingenting savnes
og begrene er fulle
og livet en lek som aldri tar slutt
en solskinnslåt når livet er flott
og folka er snille og mener godt
jeg ønsker jeg hadde en solskinnslåt
som dere kunne synge til
men vel…

Another electric night

this city is rambling on
into another electric night
and here we are
sitting side by side
along the counter of this old bar
and you're looking at me
and I'm looking at you
and I'm just about to say:
oh shall we shall we shall we
shall we go to another place?
but i don't know your name
and you don't know mine
but you're good looking and fine
yes, you're the rose in my valley
so shall we shall we shall we
shall we do something else?
let me call you sharon
oh - I think I got a hard on
but do you really care?
this city is rambling on
into another electric night
and I got to have another drink
'cause i don't think
i dare to talk to you
so give me another one
and please; brother
can you tell me that lady's name?
i mean the one over there
oh - is she really gone?
then just give me another drink
give me another one
i wanna have some fun
oh give me give me give me
give me another one
'cause i'm rambling on
into another electric night

Paying my duties

I've been paying my duties to the Department of Love
My pockets are empty and my wallet's gone
I'm jiggered and shattered and my body's growing old
And all what I had has been taken and sold

I've got no more to offer and my heart is cold
My mind is empty and my memory's gone
So please, lovers of past and future, leave me alone
There's nothing more to see here, so do move on
The audience is leaving and the applause dies down
The show is over and the lights are out
The star has left the stage and so has the clown
His cloak is tattered and worn
and his dagger has a broken blade
The armour is rusty and falling apart
and the white horse is in the abattoir
and his life has turned into a film noir

I've been paying my duties to the Department of Love
My pockets are empty and my wallet's gone
I'm jiggered and shattered and my body's growing old
And all what I had has been taken and sold
I've got no more to offer and my heart is cold

Regnskapet

Jeg har betalt min gjeld til Kjærlighetsdepartementet
lommene er tomme og lommeboka borte
jeg er utslitt og knust og kroppen min eldes
alt hva jeg eide er tatt og solgt

Jeg har ikke mere å gi og hjertet er kaldt
hodet er tomt og minnet borte
så vær så snill, elskere fra fortid og framtid
gå videre for det er ikke mere å se
publikum forlater salen og bifallet dør
forestillingen er over og lysene slukkes
stjernen har gått fra scenen og narren med
kappen er trådslitt og frynset
og dolken har et brukket blad
rustningen er rusten og i stykker
og den hvite hingsten er på vei for å slaktes
mens livet er blitt som en dyster film

Jeg har betalt min gjeld til Kjærlighetsdepartementet
lommene er tomme og lommeboka borte
jeg er utslitt og knust og kroppen min eldes
alt hva jeg eide er tatt og solgt bort
jeg har ikke mere å gi og hjertet er kaldt

Isolated in love

dust is falling down like last winter's snow
covering up all our emotions
underneath the colour of death

i want to rise
and touch the summer's heat
but i am fixed to the seat
i'm sitting on
chained to the table

our hearts they were burning like fire
but what is left is heaps of ashes
covering what we thought was love sweet love

why has our sacred garden
turned into this grave of stone?

The love game

girls are running for boys
and boys are playing with toys
we're all running like madmen
and looking like sad men
playing with tools
and acting like fools

and i don't wanna be your hero
i don't wanna be no robert deniro
i don't wanna be bad nor good
and i don't wanna be understood!

girls are planning ploys
and boys wanna be the real mccoys
girls are chasing down boys
and boys are looking at girls
we're all running like madmen
looking like sad men
playing with tools
and acting like fools

The hollow boys

down on the street
the hollow boys are lining up again
on the concrete
the lonely boys are playing their game
they wanna dance dance dance
longing for a romance
then comes a girl with a sway in her hips
oh look at that witch with lies on her lips
say the hollow boys
all of the lonely boys
see how they prance through the dance

feel the heat boiling down your spine
and shocks electrocute your foggy mind
you wanna smile smile smile
take her down the aisle
but she crushes down on your lips
brings you into some messy trips
you're a hollow boy
you're a lonely boy
and look at you how you prance

that's all right when your light is shining through
but what do you do when your black turns into blue?
you wanna get away way way
and your heart is an ashtray
the girl twitches while the slippery slips
when love is a shallow joy
and you're a hollow boy
longing to leave the dance

look at the hollow boys
all of the lonely boys
you're a hollow boy
such a lonely boy

and love is a shallow joy
for all of the hollow boys and
all of the lonely boys

The end of Santa Claus

it's the end of santa claus
when daddy loses his mask
and stands naked on the floor
when he's deprived of his pride
and the christmas trees are all on fire
and the sleigh is stuck in the quagmire
and the christmas dinner is burning in a pyre
and rudolph is upstairs
taking mummy for a ride!

yeah that's the end of santa claus
when daddy loses his mask
and stands naked on the floor
when he's deprived of his pride
and rudolph is upstairs
taking mummy for a ride!

and all the reindeers are tangled up in barbed wire
and news have come through
that the crucifixion was but a sham
and jesus had a stunt for hire
and if there was a virgin
it was not mariah
and the lion has killed the lamb
and judas was just a misguided liar

God in your pocket

so you got god in your pocket
cut him down to size
it sounds very fine and dandy
and it might come in handy
with a god pocket sized

All our houses will come down

years they are turning
and stars are burning
we stare into the starry sky
lazily wondering why
we slip and we slide
through moments of time
our past is a ghost
flashing through our mind
and what is to come
is but a shadow
a shadow we look for
but cannot find...
all our houses will have to come down
nothing lasts forever
not the stars
nor the sun
and when we rise we have to fall down
yeah down all down
and the last days of summer
will be farther behind
with the first kiss of ice
and all that we forget
when we try to remember
and when we linger
at times of departure
and all the weeping and our sentimental songs
it's all in vain
all our houses will have to come down
nothing lasts forever
not the stars nor the sun
and when we rise we have to fall down
all the way down

Days come and go

days do come and days do go
and time is passing away
people come and people die
and time is running away
the sea is beating the shore
and splashes on the stone
deep cracks are carved into skin
while the moon fades away
the blazing sun is on the rise
leaden skies and blinded eyes
and castles made of sand
wine is glowing and blood is flowing
and my mind is on the edge
fire burning, gives a warning
get out and get away!
the night is fading away
before i fall asleep
and dreams are beating my brain
black shadows and hollow eyes
ghosts who howl and weep
my brooding mind is feeding
my soul full of fear
but tears roll down and clean it away
and there comes a day
as the night fades away
and
the winter carries spring within
but nothing comes for free
no nothing comes for free

Black and thin ice

you're walking on a straight line
and you're doing it oh so fine
you are really sublime
and you rise and you shine
while i'm walking on black and thin ice
      i'm walking on black and thin ice
and what's up to you
is down to me
and where down is to you
it is where i am up
your daylight is my night
and your darkness is my light
you just follow that line
and you never decline
while i walk down a twisted line
twisting all the way down
and to get ahead
i got to turn around
yes, to get ahead
i got to turn around

Life in the city

this is life in the city
this is city life
we're living deep down in this city
our life is rock'n'roll
got blood all over my face
but whores and madonnas
wash it all away

shadows are moving in the alleys
blood is running in the gutters
and beggars are out for dinner
while we're all getting thinner
and the world is a stutter
and my mind is blue
but my soul is black

that's life in the city
and it is out of control
blood all over your face
but whores and madonnas
wash it all away

killers stalk in the shadow
stabbing the unaware in the back
flashes like lightning through the dark
and heat is boiling up the kettle
lovers hide in the nightshade
tangled up in their old game
love is turning into a hungry shark
and life is but a tiny spark

lord knows i'm a loser
everytime i'm up i'm bound to fall
but when i'm down i'm on the rise
running around   in a helluva pace
and i'm gonna make it through the day

yeah i'm gonna break it any old way
i'm gonna live it my own way!

the bars are full of madmen
blood throbbing in hot bodies
but no one pays attention
to the barmaid in her silky dress
they lost all sensation
heroes in their own imagination
breaking loose to be free

we're living in the city
and our lives are out of control
got blood all over my face
but whores and madonnas
wash it all away

Soft fools

I feel like a romance of a supreme quality has slipped through my fingers/ am I just staring into the dust now? where did the pretty eyes go/ those which begged for something I have already forgotten what was? maybe they are held captured somewhere/ perhaps they long to be set free? my body is battered but still almost without a trace of what has happened to it during this time/ some of it hidden in sand which I throw up into the air to let it be blown away with the wind and I find a skeleton buried in the sand/ I rise up and my joints creak/maybe I have been sat for too long and what happened to the wind? may I let loose a smile? a ruddy face appears and I ask it when I can let go? but a smile is the only response I get/ I should walk out the door no matter which one and out there I should hoist the sail/ I can vaguely remember that someone danced and shouted while I walked calmly and collected but it was still not enough/ there is talk about light around me but my thoughts are petrified in burnt clay before they are being heated and crumble and are swept away by time and rejected as insignificant rubbish/ soft feminine shapes in a nightly fantasy more real than flesh and blood awaken a flaming desire and our eyes are being covered in frothing white foam so why do I hesitate and what am I groping for? the rhythm of somebody else is throbbing in my own pulse/ the walls furl up and roll themselves together and dwindle away and behind them darkness pushes forward/ I want to dance ecstatic to the rhythm throbbing in the exact same beat as my pulse
only louder
harder
faster
more intense
until the walls crack open and the light seeps in/ perhaps I should try all of this out even underneath the bright light of neon but where are all the people/ are bodies and walls falling apart
and is sex
and drugs
and rock
and roll
an initiation rite in which we throw our own flesh into the fire
but can it be consumed by it?

if a death is required in order to live so let us live and let us die/ if it wasn't so hazy and blurry/ it should rather be in the middle of the blackest night/ jesus christ come and save us from this misty morning if you can

everybody is dancing faster and faster and I guess I dance along but what shall I do with all of that which is ravaging through my nights? will it just fall away like an unused hull or will it be slowly consumed and incinerated? is there a way for soft fools on which we can drive with fast cars with roaring engines and the ghosts of lou reed and nico in the backseat blindfolded? and we drive and we drive until all roads melt together into one and we faint and flow across all boundaries and we tear at the zippers until our fingers bleed and drown dream and tears and hot throbbing rhythms and wild grins/ and the road which isn't on any map or registered by GPS plunges down and down and the car is rushing ahead in neutral without gasoline until the tires explode and everything is electric white/sharp cries and desperate screams shred the darkness/ while rain pours silently down and wailing sirens come closer and blue light flashes through the night/ are there someone left out there crying for us? what happens the next morning in the antiseptic room in the huge hospital? can soft fools die or are vi condemned to grin the same sneer

over

and over again?

I ask myself as I rise up with stiff and aching limbs

and I know that fools are soft but

can be broken

down

Myke idioter

jeg føler det som om en romanse av ypperste kvalitet har runnet ut mellom fingrene mine/stirrer jeg bare ned i støv nå? hvor ble de vakre øynene av/ de som bad om noe som jeg allerede har glemt hva var? kanskje de holdes fast et sted/ kanskje de lengter etter å slippe fri? kroppen min er herjet men allikevel nesten uten et spor av det som har skjedd den under tiden/ noe av det er skjult i jord som jeg kaster opp i lufta for å la den bli blåst bort med vinden og jeg finner et skjelett nedgravd i sanden/ jeg reiser meg tungt og leddene mine knirker/ kanskje jeg har sittet for lenge og hvor ble vinden av? kan jeg slippe fri et smil? et rødt ansikt kommer til syne og jeg spør det når skal jeg slippe taket? men et smil er det eneste svaret jeg får/ jeg burde gå ut av døra likegyldig hvilken av dem og der ute skal jeg heise seil/ jeg kan huske flyktig at noen danset og skrek mens jeg gikk ganske rolig og behersket men det var allikevel ikke nok/ det snakkes om lys rundt meg men tankene mine er som størknet i leire før de varmes opp og smuldrer til støv og feies bort av tiden som ubetydelig tøv/ en kvinnes myke former i en nattlig fantasi mere virkelig enn en kropp av kjøtt og blod vekker et flammende begjær og øynene våre dekkes av frådende hvitt skum så hvorfor nøler jeg og hva famler jeg etter? en annens rytme dunker i min egen puls/ veggene krøller seg sammen og svinner bort og bak dem fosser mørket fram/ jeg vil danse ekstatisk til rytmen som svinger i nøyaktig samme takt som min puls
bare høyere
hardere
fortere
mere intenst
til veggene revner og lyset siver inn/ kanskje burde jeg forsøke alt dette selv under neonlysets skarpe skinn men hvor er alle menneskene/ er kropper og vegger i ferd med å gå i stykker
og er sex
and drugs
and rock
and roll
et innvielsesrituale der vi kaster vårt eget kjøtt i ilden
men kan det brenne opp?
hvis det kreves en død for å leve så la oss få leve og dø/ om det ikke var så tåkete og utydelig/ det burde heller vært midt på sorte natta/ jesus kristus kom og frels oss fra denne tåkete morgen om du kan

alle danser fortere og fortere og jeg danser vel med men hva skal jeg gjøre med alt det som herjer i nettene mine? vil det bare falle bort som et utbrukt skall eller vil det langsomt forbrukes og forbrennes? finnes det en vei for myke idioter som vi kan kjøre på med raske biler med brølende motorer og spøkelsene til lou reed og nico i baksetet med bind foran øynene? vi kjører og kjører til alle veier smelter sammen og vi besvimer og flyter utover

alle grenser og vi river opp glidelåser til fingrene blør og drukner drømmer og tårer i hissige rytmer og ville flir/ veien som ikke finnes på kartet og ikke registreres av GPS stuper nedover og nedover og bilen ruser fram i fri tom for drivstoff til dekkene eksploderer og alt blir elektrisk hvitt/ bitter grått og desperate rop skjærer mørket i strimler

mens regnet siler stille og uavbrutt ned oghylende sirener kommer nærmere og blålys lyner gjennom natta/er det noen igjen der ute som gråter for oss? hva skjer den neste dagen i det steriliserte rommet i det enorme sykehuset? kan myke idioter dø eller er vi dømt til å le det samme fliret

om og om igjen?

jeg spør bare i det jeg reiser meg med stive lemmer

og jeg vet at en idiot er myk

men kan brytes

ned

Faces on a parade

sometimes i sit and wonder
about death and love and hate
and i'm looking back yonder
down through the passage of time
into the blind mask of fate
and i see faces on an endless parade
moving down dark tunnels in my mind
and i remember
you and me
and cold evenings in september
and my childhood
in the countryside
and how i am rambling around
trying to survive
a city life

Johnny be dead

got a phone call the other night
someone said
your friend johnny is dead
dead oh johnny is dead
      johnny is dead
      johnny is dead and gone
he just wanted to have a good time
letting loose and feeling fine
but it was too much dope and booze
the old having a good time blues
yes that old having a good time blues
well, but johnny be dead
      johnny be dead
      johnny be dead and gone
he was just like you and me
wanted to live out his fantasy
then sometimes something goes wrong
and in the end he could not walk
and he could not talk
so they had to bring him in
then he ran away once more
(i don't know how)
and his old heart said to him
oh no johnny, oh no
and johnny he could not move
so goodbye johnny goodbye
      johnny goodbye
      johnny goodbye
fare thee well Johnny be dead and gone
left us here to sing a song
johnny be dead and gone

Lonesome roads

Sitting behind the wheel again
in my old van
Driving down these long
and lonesome roads
Don't remember
If I've been here before
On the move again
From where I lived once upon a time
Looking for a place to settle
Which I will never find

I'm a stranger in every city
Left my home a long time ago
Been driving down these lonesome roads
But I can't remember
If I've been here before
Looking for a place to settle
A place I will never find
Along these long and lonesome roads

Gods saved kings and queens

come on and let's all set sail
in search of the one and only
holy grail!
drop some acid and let it loose
let's go for peter pan and mother goose
gods saved kings and queens
so come on let's save
the goddamn whale!
show me the way and your spiritual father
and take me down to fairy town
dress me up in a nice and shiny gown
but please, don't let me stand here all alone!
take my name and my identity
take my shame and my responsibility
take it all but set me free
show me the way to your pearly gate
you know that place beyond love and hate
i go for peter pan and mother goose
drop some acid and let it loose
and we all set sail
in search of the only
holy grail!
gods saved kings and queens
so come on let's save
a goddamn whale!

Talkshow

they're talking and talking
with nothing to say
they're running and walking
with nowhere to go
sitting in chairs staring in the air
blowing bubbles with their minds

oh i am tired of watching teevee
listening to the preaching and teaching
the rattling of tongues
smiling and laughing
singing a silly song
and when the show is over
they go out drinking
chatting and shouting
calling out each other's names
rattling their tongues
singing a silly song

and the next evening
they're there again
talking and talking
with nothing to say
blowing bubbles with their minds
and rattling their tongues

You ain't got no others

we can talk about a revolution
write down a new constitution
try to find a good solution
some way out of this confusion
we may worry about the pollution
and rebel against the institution

well
you can do what you may
and i've got nothing to say
but i tell you anyway

you ain't got a chance
you just got to take it
just get up and dance
and you know you'll make it
there's no way they gonna break it

you got to throw away your crutches
and learn to walk on water
you got to stand on the ground
with your head in a cloud
and you gotta stand all alone
and you have to kill your king and goddess
and stay with your sisters and brothers
'cause you ain't got no others
you have to kill your dads and mothers
and stay with your sisters and brothers
'cause you ain't got no others

The Libella

We were all gathered around a table in the sitting room, with cups of tea placed in our hands and conversations on our tongues, when I felt that something was about to happen.

Quite right; suddenly young men stormed into the room with panic in their eyes while they shouted one on top of the others: «The Libella! The Libella is coming!»

I shuddered! A libella! An insect! Horrid images of long and thin, skeleton-like legs covered with sticky hairs rushed through my imagination. And here, of all places, where everything was so unsafe, where a word alone could have disastrous consequences and a mere thought could cause disasters!

Then a thought struck me; how do I know that a libella is an insect? Isn't it rather a political pamphlet of some sort? Am I mixing things up? And if it is an insect, how do I know what it looks like? If I don't know that, how can I see it at all, just like it would be coming in through the door?

I looked at the door precisely in that moment and saw a thin, skeleton-like leg covered with bristles coming in through the open doorway. I stared at it, transfixed, oblivious of my surroundings and the others in the room. A wedge-like head with two wide set and faceted eyes on each side of a long snout followed the leg. Its skin was light green with opaque black eyes. On its back it had huge, transparent wings with green veins running through them, forming an intricate pattern. Its hind legs were like a grasshopper's, powerful and muscular. The monster was enormous, standing more than six feet tall. In between the two bulging eyes it had a third and all three of them turned slowly towards us now. It stared at us with an inscrutable expression, assessing us.

I jumped up and pressed myself against the wall, all cold inside, overwhelmed by fear, but at the same time a voice inside me said: «Well, was it that bad, really?»

Still I began looking for weapons which I could use. Anything. We had to fight it, kill it, but how? With tea cups? Scones?

Desperately, I turned towards the others to ask for help, but to my utter astonishment I discovered that they were still sitting like nothing had happened, chatting cheerfully along, sipping tea.

«Hey!» I shouted at them, my voice cracking; «Don't you see it!? The monster? There!» I pointed at it. «Come on!» I rambled on, panicking. «We gotta do something!»

They slowly turned to look at it now. Like watching something filmed at a distance and the sound turned down to a minimum, I saw how they giggled and laughed, pointing at it like it was nothing but a harmless clown with too large shoes stumbling across the sitting room. The monster slowly approached the table and they just sat there, smiling, like they were about to offer it tea and scones.

I ran into the kitchen, searching frantically after something I could use as a weapon. I only found a glass jar and filled it with water before I ran back to the sitting room. Without aiming I threw the water against it. Most of the content had already spilled out and the few drops left didn't even wet its skin, but it was enough to avert its attention towards me and it turned slowly away from my friends. I ran back into the kitchen and filled the jar again. I threw the content at the monster aiming at a hole it had in its throat, covered with a fine web of green strands.

I was surprised.

It sat down on its hind legs and turned its head towards the ceiling and began to sing with a strange gurgling, melodious sound, like glittering bubbles bursting in the air letting delicious tones flow out.

Now I knew how to stop it! I hurried back and filled up the jar once more. When I returned to the sitting room I stopped, my mouth gaping.

The monster had vanished and a strangely beautiful woman with a light green skin was standing there instead. She looked at me with pitch black, glittering eyes. Without saying a word she commanded me only by looking at me. She wanted me to throw the water at the hole in her throat.

I protested weakly. «Wouldn't it be better - uh, if - umm, perhaps it would be more convenient if you would - I mean, if you would lie down on your back, so I could - uh - it would be more easy to...»

I felt awkwardly shy and bashful like a teenage girl from the countryside. The fear was all gone. The black lips of the strange woman curled up in a sardonic smile, gazing steadily at me. She knelt slowly down and turned her head back in a gracious arc and I felt compelled to pour water over her and the strange and oddly sensual and mesmerising sound grew stronger and it was like I was drawn into its centre, towards her, without a will of my own, oblivious of everything else.

The devil in me

My friend and I had an argument when it happened.

He angrily exclaimed:
- Oh, you Devil, you!
and I felt an energy surge up within me. That's the only way I can describe it, an upsurge, like an electric current flowing from toe to head, only it ended up around my shoulder blades. At the same time, I felt a white and blind anger racing through me, directed at my friend. The sheer power of this combined lifted me, no, inflated me, or caused me to grow. I soon felt tall and powerful, hovering above my friend, who all of a sudden appeared small and weak compared to me. His face grew pale and his eyes widened and became full of fear as he backed away from me.

I could feel how wings grew out from my shoulders and without having to look, I knew that they were leathery. And huge. Oh, the immense sense of superiority and power it gave me! I threw my head back and roared with laughter as I folded out my enormous wings. I could feel a pair of horns sprout out from my forehead while my skin turned into a blackish hue and my hands into claws.

I cackled wildly as I lifted from the ground, completely oblivious of my friend now. What time had I for mere humans? I flew up in circles, farther and farther away from the ground. I howled against the sky and turned out towards the grey ocean. When I was so far out that I could see land no more, a curious transformation took place. Although I still couldn't see myself, I just knew that I had turned into an enormous eagle. I turned my proud head and looked at my wings and quite right, they were covered with feathers, colours ranging from brown to black with some of them being white. Everything felt differently now, although I still felt enormously capable and powerful, but gone was the demonic hysteria and it was replaced by a taciturn dignity instead.

After a while, though, I felt fatigue set in. After all, I wasn't used to fly at all. This was the first time it had happened to me, to be frank. All I could see around me, however, was the grey, billowing sea. I felt I was sinking and instead of lifting me up, my wings were turning into a heavy burden. In the last moment before I helplessly crashed into the cold ocean, I saw a desolate skerry below me and with a last effort, I managed to land on this naked piece of rock, sprayed all wet and slippery by the salty breakers crashing down upon it. As I touched ground, my wings disappeared and I was merely a poor and lost human being, stuck on this rock in the middle of the ocean.

By the Beyond

There is a grapevine hedge down our road and it has Voices in it, whispering after dark, claiming that life here is no good. That isn't true, though. Life here is very good and we all agree on that. We have a lot of fun all the time. Just ask the twins, for instance. They stick together all the time, chit-chatting about this and that and although it is only Laura laughing, I am sure Betty enjoys it, too. Yes, I know she always looks a little downcast and what with her being dumb and all and never getting away from her sister, it surely can be challenging, but Laura is always full of it. Full of fun, I mean. Just the way she teases Betty's doll, which isn't really a doll, come to think of it.

Or rather, I'd better not think of it.

…

I also understand that some may react negatively when they see Headless Annie for the first time, but I think that it's not just to her. It isn't her fault, is it? And she takes very good care of her head all the time so she isn't really headless then, is she? It is always with her and she lets it rest on the cushioned bench she usually sits on. It is a nice head, too. Nothing wrong with it, really. It just doesn't sit on Annie's neck, that's all.

And there is nothing wrong with Moonboy, either. Nothing seriously wrong, at least. Yes, I admit that one gets a little uneasy the way he just sits there, staring. It can be a bit unnerving, especially at the end of the day, but it isn't so easy for him, either, since he hasn't any ears, so he can't hear you, anyway. No one knows what he is thinking of since he hasn't told anyone about it. And yes, that human skull he always carries around, just like Annie and her head… Oh well, he used to know Leopold Ragdol and he was probably the only one who never ran after him, throwing sticks and stones, so he must be nice enough, don't you think? I try to think so, at least.

But it is getting dark now so I think the fun time is over for today. I wouldn't be sitting here when the Wailers pass by. You don't know who they are? You wouldn't like to know, either, I can assure you. No one does know, actually. I think they are Condemned Ones, if you know what I mean. You don't? Well, it is rather difficult to explain then, but it is like they are lost and have to stumble down our street riding on their stupid stick-horses, dressed in polka dot prison gear, growling and wailing as they move towards the Beyond.

Hush! Don't you hear them now? The moon is coming up soon, too, and Moonboy... oh, we better go inside! Hurry!

Leopold Ragdol

I should have understood it from his name, but I was only a child myself, and that was what I thought he was, too. Besides, I only knew him as Leopold then.

I pitied him the first time I saw him. All the other children screamed and laughed and pointed at him. I don't recall if the first stone was thrown already then, that day when he came humping down our street for the first time. It was in July and so late in the afternoon that the shadows had grown long and deep. He was nothing but a movement among the darkest of the shadows which groped like black, inky fingers across the cracked pavement. Then he humped out into the light.

Yes, humped. It cannot be described with another word the way he moved. How else can you move if you only have one leg? You hump.

Oh, it was not like he had lost a leg. No, his torso grew right up from this huge leg he had and he never had more than that one leg. That was how he was created, by some ill fate or by an evil twist of a Creator's mind, like a sick joke, maybe. I don't know. I just felt this wave of sadness surge through me seeing him humping down the street.

Later, I got used to seeing his odd form humping along. I always stood there with tears burning in the corners of my eyes, helplessly watching the poor creature move so awkwardly along, with a tail of screaming and laughing children after him. I wished I could run after him, in secret, maybe, to stop and talk to him when we both were out of sight from the others, just to tell him that we were not all like they were, that there is still some good in this world, but I did not dare. I was afraid, yes, I was afraid of becoming another prey running in front of the wild horde. So poor Leopold humped on alone, until he came to the end of our street, which also marked the end of our world. No one we knew had ever been into the Beyond, no one but Leopold, but then, no one really knew him, did they?

I said I wished I could have talked to him, but how do you talk to someone who has no face? Oh, he had, but not a face like a face should be. First of all, there was no mouth in it. And his eyes were like two blind buttons sewed on. If I had dared to go after him and tried to talk, he would not have been able to hear a word, either, because he had no ears.

It was months later when I finally understood and the odd thing was that it was the very same day I heard his full name pronounced. It was only then I noticed the tiny stitches at the back of his head and I understood that he really was Leonard the Ragdoll. It was also the day he never returned from Beyond.

Four Hares In a Boat

The four Hares were not really keen on fishing. To be exact, they were not interested in anything at all which had to do with fish or fisheries or angling or anything related to it. Hares do not eat fish.

But then again, what do you do when you come across a good boat which looks like it is perfect for fishing? You get curious, of course.

Well, some do. Jack Hare was one of those.

- Come on guys! He called out to the others when they saw the boat in the middle of the wood. - Let us jump on board!

-I am not willing to do anything of the sort, Bill Hare grumbled. He had a slight stomach ache and was not in any mood for adventures at all, and far from any which involved a boat. Peter and Bob Hare felt insecure about it, but they were normally easily persuaded and Jack Hare knew it, so he directed his enthusiasm towards them.

-Bob? Peter? You are with me, aren't you?

-Oh well, I don't... Peter began. Bob looked behind him at Bill to get some support, but Bill had demonstratively turned his back on it all.

The boat looked like how a boat normally looks like, with a prow and aft and keel and all, but it seemed a bit odd in the middle of a forest, without any body of water in sight, be it still or running, salt or sweet. Still, everyone could see it was a well built boat.

Jack climbed on board and moved towards the prow where he eagerly sniffed around.

- Oh, it smells really good! he shouted to the others.

- Does it now? Peter said, wary. A loud and contemptuous snort was heard from Bill. Bob looked nervously at him, obviously in doubt about what to do.

- Come on now! Jack pleaded. - We're just having a look at it. Nothing can happen! We are in the middle of the forest, aren't we? The boat cannot go anywhere!

He laughed and shook his head at the thought. Bob and Peter looked at each other and shrugged their shoulders and sighed. Bob was the first one to climb on board and Jack offered him a paw while Peter gave him a push.

- Come on, Bill! Jack shouted. - Are you going to grow roots or something? Jump on board now!

Bill grunted something intelligible but he gave grudgingly in and climbed on board, but moved to the aft and sat demonstratively down on the thwart. That was when it happened. The boat moved.

They all froze.

The hull heaved itself like it was rolling on a wave and all four grabbed hold of the gunwale.

Jack was the first to discover the legs. The boat had four huge legs sticking out from the hull. Hairy human legs.

- What the...? Jack exclaimed and gulped.

The legs began to move. The boat walked, but it walked backwards. Jack grabbed hold of the prow, like he wanted to force the boat to move in the right direction. Peter who sat behind him, closed his eyes and looked down.

-I knew it, I knew it! We should never have done this! I knew it! he whispered to himself in a weak whimper.

- I wonder if... Bob was muttering behind him again. - I just wonder if we couldn't...

- What? Couldn't do what? Jack snarled impatiently back.

- Well, jump off... Bob continued.

But of course! And they all got up. Or they tried to get up but it was like they were glued to the thwarts. They couldn't move. They were stuck.

Bill was the only one who hadn't bothered to try even. He sat with his hands folded over his aching stomach and he mumbled under his breath:

- Oh yes. Naturally. Of course. A boat. Indeed. Hah!

And the boat continued walking with the four Hares on board and there was nothing they could do about it. It moved towards the Beyond and that was the last anyone heard about them.

The artwork that inspired this story, by Shelly Wyn-De-Bank.

No time to die

I got no time to die
dying is for suckers
so hang down your head
if you will Tom Dooley
hang down your head and cry
I am too busy living
got no time for dying
and even Christ said
we'd better deal with life and the living
so let the dead mourn the dead like he said
while we got a life to live
so we better live it until the day we die
and if your days are full of pain and sorrow
you better laugh till you cry
because there is a tomorrow
but we don't know what it brings
it might be our gain or more of the pain
we just don't know
so keep your head up and run for the hills
but don't forget
to pay your bills

The Land of Transition

Have you heard of The Land of Transition? It lies where the nation states become fuzzy and shift from either one to the other. It is where cultures and languages shamelessly go to bed with one another. We who are from that land, are a little bit of something and of anything in between and we live in the shift between the fixed and decided and what is writ into law and rules and what is left unspoken. That is exactly where The Land of Transition is, in the cracks in between. It is neither this nor that and even more so, and so are we who hail from that land.

We are not living in a transitional state, though, sat in the waiting room of the national states, anxiously and eagerly awaiting for any nation state to call out: Next, please! No, we are born and have grown up in The Land of Transition, the zone somewhere in between the ambiguous and the unambiguous, and even if we should emigrate, we will always bring our origin with us. We are proud citizens of The Land of Transition, which is a land without land and thus, it will be forever fixed in its original state and we who come from that land, will always be somewhere in between everywhere, neither here nor there.

I wish

I wish I could give you words of love and light and hope
full of inspiration and how to cope
But as I search high and low
I only find visions of darkness and despair
Of loss and grievances and how I fell down a stair
Crawling through tunnels towards the light
Which I hope is at the end of the night
I long for a world somewhere beyond
A place filled with laughter, dance and a song
Wine and women and all that belong
Oh how I wish I could fill your minds
With images of joy and sheer delight
I wish life wasn't filled with so many rainy days
Damp clothes and cold feet
I wish
I wish for an eternal spring
When everybody laugh and children sing
And there's a girl on a swing
Nothing hides under the bed
And everyone is rested and well fed
I wish life was complete
From the start and nothing was missing
From the beginning to the end
I wish for all of that to come true
But then what can I do
I have to take what I find
I cannot lie or pretend
And I think to myself
Maybe that's how we learn what love is
Through pain and grief and loss and defeat
Maybe that's the only way the heart can grow
Maybe it has to be cast into the fire
To come out pure as gold
Cleansed from yearning and desire
With nothing left but hope for ourselves
And love for the other

From dead bodies to hope

I'm thinking of dead bodies. I'm thinking of summer. I'm thinking of distorted faces filled with blind fear behind a machine gun spitting out death. I'm thinking of a chaos filled with unpleasant hard stares from dead black eyes and pale skin behind explosions blowing up the silence to smithereens. Shards of broken mirrors.

I'm thinking of sea water clear as crystal over shiny white sand. I'm thinking of sandy beaches encircled by rocks, dark and glistening from the last flow. I'm thinking of yellowish dry and withered grass. I'm thinking of the small bodies of boys skipping between the rocks jumping over the dried up seagulls' nests from last year, running and laughing at the wide expanse of the glittering ocean towards the horizon. I'm thinking of the sweet scent of newly cut hay stacked up to dry. I'm thinking of everything those kids didn't know about yet.

I'm thinking about being drunk on booze. I'm thinking of the nausea and retchings which have to be forced back for every new sip of the bottle. I'm thinking of the raw liquor which rolls slowly down the throat like a flaming ball of fire and I'm thinking of how it burns like ice. I'm thinking of the hot impulses rocking through a feverish brain. I'm thinking of the outlines slowly being erased, becoming blurry shining with a vapid light. I'm thinking of the washed-out reflections in the bottles. I'm thinking of the closeness and contact and the rushing overconfidence through the pulsating blood. I'm thinking of the burning blows of hard fists. I'm thinking of blood flowing and running. I'm thinking of grimaces washed out by salty tears and sticky dribble. I'm thinking of the bittersweet vomit on the green grass. I'm thinking of soiled clothes. I'm thinking of wet and warm puke flowing over my fingers. I'm thinking of the solitude in a dark night and the cold sheen from lonely street lamps. I'm thinking of black and humid asphalt. I'm thinking of being alone with all knowledge about lies and sins, bitter defeat and splintered illusions, trampled down underneath muddy soles. I'm thinking of a dark laughter in a black night.

I'm thinking of deep eyes vibrating electric dark for you. I'm thinking of tender hands discovering your body. I'm thinking of words whispered to you and meant only for you. I'm thinking of time slowly rotating around its own axis. I'm thinking of the heat in the dark room. I'm thinking of the thrusts revealing the room in blinding flashes. I'm thinking of tears covering all smiles with a thin film. I'm thinking of quivering lips. I'm thinking of the world slowly disintegrating and trembling before it turns towards you. I'm thinking of shiny eyes and glittering tears and a soft mouth smiling and a warm body succumbing to yours.

I'm thinking of life and pulsating rhythms. I'm thinking of everything in a state of incessant change. I'm thinking of ephemeral touches. I'm thinking of smiles withdrawing dissolved in tears instead of dying in a hardened grimace.
I'm thinking of hope.

Tanker om alt fra døde kropper til håp

Jeg tenker på lik. Jeg tenker på sommer. Jeg tenker på fordreide ansikter som lyser av blind skrekk bak et dødsprutende maskingevær. Jeg tenker på et kaos av stikkende, kullsorte øyne og hvit hud bak lynende eksplosjoner som flerrer opp stillheten i tusener skarpe splinter. Biter av knuste speil.

Jeg tenker på en krystallklar sjø over lysende hvit sandbunn. Jeg tenker på hvite skjellsandstrender omkranset av steiner, mørke og matt glinsende etter siste flo. Jeg tenker på vissent og gulbrunt gress. Jeg tenker på små guttekropper som sprang mellom steinene og hoppet over fjorårets visne måsereir og løp og lo mot havet som strakte seg glitrende ut mot horisonten. Jeg tenker på den søte lukten av nyslått høy på hesjer. Jeg tenker på alt som disse barna ennå ikke visste noe om.

Jeg tenker på brennevinsrus. Jeg tenker på kvalmen og brekningene som må tvinges tilbake for hver ny slurk av flaska. Jeg tenker på den rå spriten som ruller langsomt lik en flammende ildkule nedover strupen og jeg tenker på den kalde brannen i magen. Jeg tenker på de heite impulsene som gynger gjennom en febersyk hjerne. Jeg tenker på konturene som sakte hviskes ut, blir slørete og lyser svakt. Jeg tenker på det matte gjenskinnet som reflekteres i flaskene. Jeg tenker på nærheten og kontakten og det brusende overmotet som skyller gjennom blodet. Jeg tenker på de sviende slagene. Jeg tenker på blodet som renner og renner. Jeg tenker på grimaser som vaskes utydelige av salte tårer og seigt spytt. Jeg tenker på det bittersøte oppkastet som spruter utover det grønne gresset. Jeg tenker på de nedsølte klærne. Jeg tenker på vått og varmt spy som renner over fingrene. Jeg tenker på ensomheten i en mørk natt og det kalde skinnet fra enslige gatelykter. Jeg tenker på svart og fuktig asfalt. Jeg tenker på det å være alene med all viten om løgner og synder, bitre nederlag og splintrede drømmer, tråkket i stykker under gjørmete skosåler. Jeg tenker på mørk latter i en sort natt. Jeg tenker på dype øyne som sitrer elektrisk mørkt for deg. Jeg tenker på myke hender som oppdager kroppen din. Jeg tenker på ord og tanker som hviskes bare for deg og som er ment bare for deg. Jeg tenker på tiden som dreier rundt seg selv i en langsom spiral. Jeg tenker på heten i det mørke rommet. Jeg tenker på støtene som avdekker rommet i blendende lysglimt. Jeg tenker på tårer som legger en myk hinne over alle smil. Jeg tenker på sitrende lepper. Jeg tenker på verden som langsomt går i oppløsning og som vibrerer og skjelver før den vender seg innover mot deg. Jeg tenker på strålende øyne og glitrende tårer og på en myk munn som smiler og en varm kropp som gir seg over til din. Jeg tenker på liv og på pulserende rytmer. Jeg tenker på alt som er i uopphørlig forandring. Jeg tenker på flyktig berøring. Jeg tenker på smil som trekker seg tilbake oppløst i tårer i stedet for å dø hen i en stivnet grimase. Jeg tenker på håp.

Spring Ballad

It's spring! It's spring! It's spring!
and the junkies come forward
and daddy comes home
from prison!

It's spring! It's spring! It's spring!
and soon our bodies will break free
from cold and clammy
restrictions!

It's spring! It's spring! It's spring!
and deep down inside me
I feel this sore and strange little
emotion!

Vårvise

Det er vår! Det er vår! Det er vår!
og de narkomane kommer frem
og pappa vender hjem
fra fengsel!

Det er vår! Det er vår! Det er vår!
og snart så bryter kroppen frem
fra klærnes kalde, klamme
stengsel!

Det er vår! Det er vår! Det er vår!
og inni meg så kjenner jeg
en sår og rar liten
lengsel!

Wilfred Hildonen

Wilfred Hildonen was born on a Sunday, the 15th of March 1953, by the banks of the river Tana which forms the border between Norway and Finland, as far north as the countries go, in the Arctic zone. He is mainly of Sami and Finnish ancestry, the Sami being the indigenous people of Northern Europe, living across and divided by four nation states - Norway, Sweden, Finland and Russia. Aside from this he is also partly Karelian, which is a Russian republic today, the home of Kalevala, the Finnish national epos. His Karelian ancestors were known to be among the best rune-singers, wandering storytellers who brought the ancient tales of Kalevala down through the ages. Through his paternal grandmother, he is also part Romani, a people akin to the Roma, otherwise known as gypsies.

He was born in the ruins of WWII, as the retiring German occupants burnt down everything up there, so although eight years had passed, he lived his first months in an earthen dwelling, built out of dried peat, before his family moved into a cottage with one room and a kitchen. He has been on the move since then and has lived for shorter and longer periods in Greece, Spain, Sweden, Finland, Portugal and Brazil. He recently moved from the Åland Islands, an autonomous region of Finland, located in the middle of the Baltic Ocean, to a small town in Sweden.

He has been working as an editorial cartoonist and illustrator since 1992, mostly for the largest Finnish daily in the Swedish language, Hufvudstadsbladet. Aside from that he paints, mostly abstract, and he writes and so far he has published one book in Norwegian; Livet - kort og godt or Life In Short. One of the stories here, Four Hares in a Boat, was inspired by an artwork of the English artist Shelly Wyn-De-Bank, and it has been sent on a local radio station based outside London, read by the English actor Tony Ffitch. The poem Spring Ballad/Vårvise was included in an international project initiated by Ron Whitehead called From The Ancestors: Poems and Prayers for Future Generations. He also created the cover art for that project.

He is fluent in four languages; Norwegian, English, Swedish and Portuguese. He also understands Danish and some German and Spanish, but very little Finnish.

Also Available From
Cajun Mutt Press

Owls in Hot Rods with Pink Elephants and Dead Bats
by James D. Casey IV
ISBN 978-1548246228

Absurd
by R. Bremner
ISBN 978-1725983618

Dark Linings
by Joanne Olivieri
ISBN 978-1727550375

Haight
By Red Focks
ISBN 978-1726471251

Juggernaut Fuzz
By Ryan Quinn Flanagan
ISBN 978-1730783333

Isomorphic
by James D. Casey IV
ISBN 978-1724001146

This Many Years After The War
by Matthew Borczon
ISBN 978-1731194220

Wild Rose Country
by R. Keith
ISBN 978-0578439815

Detritus Of The Drunken Night
by Ian Lewis Copestick
ISBN 978-1092511148

Dreams Of Mongolia
by Will Mayo
ISBN 978-1093504101

Requiem for a Robot Dog
by Lauren Scharhag
ISBN 978-1099369032

Around the bend
By R. Keith
ISBN 978-1696088923

Miles of Sky Above Us, Miles of Earth Below
by Steve Denehan
ISBN 978-0578559964

Where Hot Rods Ride
By Mendes Biondo
ISBN 978-1072842316

9999
by R. Keith
ISBN 978-1077978430

Stick Figure Opera
by Howie Good
ISBN 978-1702328791

Hoodoo Voodoo
by Will Mayo
ISBN 978-1711010427

Safer Behind Popcorn
by Sean Hanrahan
ISBN 978-1652008699

Unwritten Words That Slide Down The Wall
by James D. Casey IV
ISBN 978-1099516672

Sharks & Butterflies
by John D. Robinson
ISBN 978-0578650982

Fracture Point
by Rani Whitehead
ISBN 978-0578632865

Written in Darkness
by Anthony Watkins
ISBN 978-0578734217

The Shells Encasing Our Nothingness
by Will Mayo
ISBN 978-0578757278

Life,
by R. Keith
ISBN 979-8690813864

The Queen & Her Devil: A Sacred Journey Through Love and Contracts
by Rani Whitehead
ISBN 978-0578796505

Oracles froma Strange Fire
by Merritt Waldon & Ron Whitehead
ISBN 978-0578823492

I Hear Your Music Playing Night and Day
by Dave O'Leary
ISBN 978-1639011636

A Screaming Place
by Brian Rihlmann
ISBN 978-1-63972-391-1

Bone Talking
by Will Mayo
ISBN 978-1685649166

The Adventures of Brain Man
by Ron Whitehead
ISBN 978-1685648886

Somniloquy & Trauma in the Knottseau Well
by Tim Heerdink
ISBN 978-1684898589

cajunmuttpress@gmail.com

https://cajunmuttpress.wordpress.com/

https://www.facebook.com/CajunMuttPress/

https://www.instagram.com/cmp_publishing/

https://twitter.com/MuttCajun

Made in the USA
Coppell, TX
26 September 2022